McD........

by Iain Gray

Lang**Syne**

PUBLISHING

WRITING *to* REMEMBER

Lang**Syne**

PUBLISHING

WRITING *to* REMEMBER

Strathclyde Business Centre
120 Carstairs Street, Glasgow G40 4JD
Tel: 0141 554 9944 Fax: 0141 554 9955
E-mail: info@scottish-memories.co.uk
www.langsyneshop.co.uk

Design by Dorothy Meikle
Printed by Hay Nisbet Press, Glasgow
© Lang Syne Publishers Ltd 2008

ISBN 1-85217-266-5

McDermott

MOTTO:
Honour and virtue.

CREST:
A demi-lion rampant
holding a sceptre.

NAME variations include:
MacDiarmada *(Gaelic)*,
MacDermot, MacDormand,
MacDermot, McDermid,
McDermott, McDermitt,
McDermont, McDiarmid,
McKermott, Darmody,
Dermody, Dermott,
Kermode, O'Moroney,
McRony, Mulrooney, Roe.

Chapter one:
Origins of Irish surnames

**According to an old saying, there are two types of Irish –
those who actually are Irish and those who wish they were.**

This sentiment is only one example of the allure that the
high romance and drama of the proud nation's history holds
for thousands of people scattered across the world today.

It's a sad fact, however, that the vast majority of Irish
surnames are found far beyond Irish shores, rather than on
the Emerald Isle itself.

The population stood at around eight million souls in
1841, but today it stands at fewer than six million.

This is mainly a tragic consequence of the potato
famine, also known as the Great Hunger, which devastated
Ireland between 1845 and 1849.

The Irish peasantry had become almost wholly reliant
for basic sustenance on the potato, first introduced from the
Americas in the seventeenth century.

When the crop was hit by a blight, at least 800,000
people starved to death while an estimated two million
others were forced to seek a new life far from their native
shores – particularly in America, Canada, and Australia.

The effects of the potato blight continued until about
1851, by which time a firm pattern of emigration had
become established.

Ireland's loss, however, was to the gain of the countries in which the immigrants settled, contributing enormously, as their descendants do today, to the well being of the nations in which their forefathers settled.

But those who were forced through dire circumstance to establish a new life in foreign parts never forgot their roots, or the proud heritage and traditions of the land that gave them birth.

Nor do their descendants.

It is a heritage that is inextricably bound up in the colourful variety of Irish names themselves – and the origin and history of these names forms an integral part of the vibrant drama that is the nation's history, one of both glorious fortune and tragic misfortune.

This history is well documented, and one of the most important and fascinating of the earliest sources are *The Annals of the Four Masters*, compiled between 1632 and 1636 by four friars at the Franciscan Monastery in County Donegal.

Compiled from earlier sources, and purporting to go back to the Biblical Deluge, much of the material takes in the mythological origins and history of Ireland and the Irish.

This includes tales of successive waves of invaders and settlers such as the Fomorians, the Partholonians, the Nemedians, the Fir Bolgs, the Tuatha De Danann, and the Laigain.

Of particular interest are the *Milesian Genealogies*,

because the majority of Irish clans today claim a descent from either Heremon, Ir, or Heber – three of the sons of Milesius, a king of what is now modern day Spain.

These sons invaded Ireland in the second millennium B.C, apparently in fulfilment of a mysterious prophecy received by their father.

This Milesian lineage is said to have ruled Ireland for nearly 3,000 years, until the island came under the sway of England's King Henry II in 1171 following what is known as the Cambro-Norman invasion.

This is an important date not only in Irish history in general, but for the effect the invasion subsequently had for Irish surnames.

'Cambro' comes from the Welsh, and 'Cambro-Norman' describes those Welsh knights of Norman origin who invaded Ireland.

But they were invaders who stayed, inter-marrying with the native Irish population and founding their own proud dynasties that bore Cambro-Norman names such as Archer, Barbour, Brannagh, Fitzgerald, Fitzgibbon, Fleming, Joyce, Plunkett, and Walsh – to name only a few.

These 'Cambro-Norman' surnames that still flourish throughout the world today form one of the three main categories in which Irish names can be placed – those of Gaelic-Irish, Cambro-Norman, and Anglo-Irish.

Previous to the Cambro-Norman invasion of the twelfth century, and throughout the earlier invasions and settlement of those wild bands of sea rovers known as the Vikings in the eighth and ninth centuries, the population of the island was relatively small, and it was normal for a person to be identified through the use of only a forename.

But as population gradually increased and there were many more people with the same forename, surnames were adopted to distinguish one person, or one community, from another.

Individuals identified themselves with their own particular tribe, or 'tuath', and this tribe – that also became known as a clann, or clan – took its name from some distinguished ancestor who had founded the clan.

The Gaelic-Irish form of the name Kelly, for example, is Ó Ceallaigh, or O'Kelly, indicating descent from an original 'Ceallaigh', with the 'O' denoting 'grandson of.' The name was later anglicised to Kelly.

The prefix 'Mac' or 'Mc', meanwhile, as with the clans of the Scottish Highlands, denotes 'son of.'

Although the Irish clans had much in common with their Scottish counterparts, one important difference lies in what are known as 'septs', or branches, of the clan.

Septs of Scottish clans were groups who often bore an entirely different name from the clan name but were under the clan's protection.

In Ireland, septs were groups that shared the same name and who could be found scattered throughout the four provinces of Ulster, Leinster, Munster, and Connacht.

The 'golden age' of the Gaelic-Irish clans, infused as their veins were with the blood of Celts, pre-dates the Viking invasions of the eighth and ninth centuries and the Norman invasion of the twelfth century, and the sacred heart of the country was the Hill of Tara, near the River Boyne, in County Meath.

Known in Gaelic as 'Teamhar na Rí', or Hill of Kings, it was the royal seat of the 'Ard Rí Éireann', or High King of Ireland, to whom the petty kings, or chieftains, from the island's provinces were ultimately subordinate.

It was on the Hill of Tara, beside a stone pillar known as the Irish 'Lia Fáil', or Stone of Destiny, that the High Kings were inaugurated and, according to legend, this stone would emit a piercing screech that could be heard all over Ireland when touched by the hand of the rightful king.

The Hill of Tara is today one of the island's main tourist attractions.

Opposition to English rule over Ireland, established in the wake of the Cambro-Norman invasion, broke out frequently and the harsh solution adopted by the powerful forces of the Crown was to forcibly evict the native Irish from their lands.

These lands were then granted to Protestant colonists, or 'planters', from Britain.

Many of these colonists, ironically, came from Scotland and were the descendants of the original 'Scotti', or 'Scots', who gave their name to Scotland after migrating there in the fifth century A.D., from the north of Ireland.

Colonisation entailed harsh penal laws being imposed on the majority of the native Irish population, stripping them practically of all of their rights.

The Crown's main bastion in Ireland was Dublin and its environs, known as the Pale, and it was the dispossessed peasantry who lived outside this Pale, desperately striving to eke out a meagre living.

It was this that gave rise to the modern-day expression of someone or something being 'beyond the pale'.

Attempts were made to stamp out all aspects of the ancient Gaelic-Irish culture, to the extent that even to bear a Gaelic-Irish name was to invite discrimination.

This is why many Gaelic-Irish names were anglicised with, for example, and noted above, Ó Ceallaigh, or O'Kelly, being anglicised to Kelly.

Succeeding centuries have seen strong revivals of Gaelic-Irish consciousness, however, and this has led to many families reverting back to the original form of their name, while the language itself is frequently found on the fluent tongues of an estimated 90,000 to 145,000 of the island's population.

Ireland's turbulent history of religious and political strife is one that lasted well into the twentieth century, a landmark century that saw the partition of the island into the twenty-six counties of the independent Republic of

Ireland, or Eire, and the six counties of Northern Ireland, or Ulster.

Dublin, originally founded by Vikings, is now a vibrant and truly cosmopolitan city while the proud city of Belfast is one of the jewels in the crown of Ulster.

It was Saint Patrick who first brought the light of Christianity to Ireland in the fifth century A.D.

Interpretations of this Christian message have varied over the centuries, often leading to bitter sectarian conflict – but the many intricately sculpted Celtic Crosses found all over the island are symbolic of a unity that crosses the sectarian divide.

It is an image that fuses the 'old gods' of the Celts with Christianity.

All the signs from the early years of this new millennium indicate that sectarian strife may soon become a thing of the past – with the Irish and their many kinsfolk across the world, be they Protestant or Catholic, finding common purpose in the rich tapestry of their shared heritage.

Chapter two:

Warriors for freedom

**A clan whose history is inextricably entwined with the
turbulent history of Ireland itself, the McDermotts of
today can trace their roots back through the dim mists
of time to the ancient province of Connacht.**

One of the original native Irish clans the McDermotts, in
all the variety of spellings of the name, shared a common
descent with the Ó Conchobhairs, or O'Connors, from
Tadhg O'Connor, king of the province from 925 to 956 A.D.

Although a branch of the O'Connor kings of Connacht,
the McDermotts went on to forge their own unique identity
through what became the two septs, or branches, of
McDermott Roe and the McDermott kings of Moylurg.

The tenth century Tadhg O'Connor had two sons,
Maolruanaidh and Conor, who agreed that Maolruanaidh
would be granted his own lands in the territory of Moylurg
– in the north of the present day County Roscommon – on
condition that he surrender all claims to the O'Connor
kingship.

It was in Moylurg that Maolruanaidh's descendants
would rule until the late sixteenth century.

The name 'Moylurg' itself is firmly rooted in ancient
myth and legend.

Known in Gaelic as Magh Luirg an Dagda, or 'the plain

of the tracks of Dagda', it referred to the Celtic god Dagda.

Tradition holds that the 'tracks of Dagda' refer to the marks left on the land by his inordinately large penis being dragged behind him.

Whatever the doubtful veracity of this, what is known for certain is that it was through Maolruanaidh that the proud Clan Mulrooney took its name, while it was through one of his grandsons, Diarmuid Ó Maolruanaidh, king of Moylurg from 1124 to 1159, that the McDermotts took their name.

'Diarmuid', 'Dermot', or 'Dermott', meanwhile, is thought to signify either 'great warrior', 'free man', or 'free of jealously'.

The genesis of the McDermott Roe sept lies in a particularly brutal incident.

This involved the deliberate blinding of Dermot, a grandson of an early thirteenth century king of Moylurg, by Aedh O'Connor, king of Connacht.

It would appear that the hapless Dermot may have had a legitimate claim on the kingship and, to prevent this, O'Connor blinded him in 1266.

But this was no senseless act of violence.

Under a law known as tanistry a person was prevented from succeeding to kingship if he was severely physically impaired – such as blind.

Dermot, who became known as Dermot Dall, with 'Dall' signifying 'blind' was compensated by being given lands for him and his descendants, and it was from

McDermott Roe, one of his grandsons, that the McDermott Roe sept took its name.

As the hereditary marshals of Connacht, with responsibility for raising and co-ordinating the province's military forces, the McDermotts of Moylurg played an important role, while another mark of their distinction was that they were entitled to preside at the inauguration ceremonies of the O'Connor kings.

Towards the end of the twelfth century their fighting prowess was tested to the full as they, along with other native Irish clans, attempted to resist a powerful onslaught by invaders from across the sea.

The attempt would ultimately fail, and the following centuries would be marked by a series of rebellions against those who had occupied the island and enforced their rule.

Twelfth century Ireland was far from being a unified nation, split up as it was into territories ruled over by squabbling chieftains who ruled as kings in their own right – and this inter-clan rivalry worked to the advantage of the invaders.

In a series of bloody conflicts one chieftain, or king, would occasionally gain the upper hand over his rivals, and by 1156 the most powerful was Muirchertach MacLochlainn, king of the O'Neills.

Rory O'Connor, king of the province of Connacht, opposed him but he increased his power and influence by allying himself with Dermot MacMurrough, king of Leinster.

MacLochlainn and MacMurrough were aware that the main key to the kingdom of Ireland was the thriving trading port of Dublin that had been established by invading Vikings, or Ostmen, in 852 A.D.

Dublin was taken by the combined forces of the Leinster and Connacht kings, but when MacLochlainn died the Dubliners rose up in revolt and overthrew the unpopular MacMurrough.

A triumphant Rory O'Connor entered Dublin and was later inaugurated as Ard Rí, but MacMurrough was not one to humbly accept defeat.

He appealed for help from England's Henry II in unseating O'Connor, an act that was to radically affect the future course of Ireland's fortunes.

The English monarch agreed to help MacMurrough, but distanced himself from direct action by delegating his Norman subjects in Wales with the task.

These ambitious and battle-hardened barons and knights had first settled in Wales following the Norman Conquest of England in 1066 and, with an eye on rich booty, plunder, and lands, were only too eager to obey their sovereign's wishes and furnish MacMurrough with aid.

MacMurrough crossed the Irish Sea to Bristol, where he rallied powerful barons such as Robert Fitzstephen and Maurice Fitzgerald to his cause, along with Gilbert de Clare, Earl of Pembroke.

The mighty Norman war machine soon moved into

action, and so fierce and disciplined was their onslaught on
the forces of Rory O'Connor and his allies that by 1171 they
had re-captured Dublin and other strategically important
territories.

Henry II began to take cold feet over the venture,
realising that he may have created a rival in the form of a
separate Norman kingdom in Ireland.

Accordingly, he landed on the island, near Waterford, at
the head of a large army in October of 1171 with the aim of
curbing the power of his Cambro-Norman barons.

Protracted war between the king and his barons was
averted, however, when the barons submitted to the royal
will, promising homage and allegiance in return for holding
the territories they had conquered in the king's name.

Henry also received the reluctant submission and
homage of many of the Irish chieftains.

English dominion over Ireland was ratified through the
Treaty of Windsor of 1175, under the terms of which Rory
O'Connor, for example, was allowed to rule territory
unoccupied by the Normans in the role of a vassal of the
king.

Further waves of English settlers descended on the
island and the Crown's grip intensified.

Ireland gradually came to be composed of the territories
of the privileged and powerful Norman barons and their
retainers, the Ireland of the disaffected native Irish such as
the McDermotts who held lands unoccupied by the

Normans, and the Pale – comprised of Dublin itself and a substantial area of its environs ruled over by an English elite.

An indication of the harsh treatment meted out to the native Irish can be found in a desperate plea sent to Pope John XII by Roderick O'Carroll of Ely, Donald O'Neil of Ulster, and a number of other Irish chieftains in 1318.

They stated: 'As it very constantly happens, whenever an Englishman, by perfidy or craft, kills an Irishman, however noble, or however innocent, be he clergy or layman, there is no penalty or correction enforced against the person who may be guilty of such wicked murder.

'But rather the more eminent the person killed and the higher rank which he holds among his own people, so much more is the murderer honoured and rewarded by the English, and not merely by the people at large, but also by the religious and bishops of the English race.'

This appeal to the Pope had little effect on what became the increasingly harsh policy of the occupying English Crown against the native Irish such as the McDermotts.

But resistance did not only take the form of written appeals.

Chapter three:

Risings and rebellion

One of the sparks that set off the flames of rebellion against the English Crown was a policy started during the reign from 1491 to 1547 of Henry VIII, whose Reformation effectively outlawed the established Roman Catholic faith throughout his dominions, of 'planting', or settling loyal Protestants on land held by the native Irish.

This policy continued throughout the subsequent reigns of Elizabeth I, James I (James VI of Scotland), and Charles I.

In 1599, allied with the O'Rourkes and the Healys, the McDermotts of Moylurg inflicted a resounding defeat on an English force commanded by Sir Conyers Clifford in what was known as the battle of the Curlews.

The battle was fought during the Nine Years War, from 1594 to 1603, and the rebel leaders, known as the Confederate Chiefs, later received aid from King Philip III of Spain in the form of a Spanish invasion force that landed at Kinsale in 1601 under the command of Don Juan del Águila.

Joined by a rebel army from Ulster, in the north, it was defeated following the siege of Kinsale, and Águila surrendered to Lord Mountjoy, Queen Elizabeth's Lord Deputy for Ireland.

The rebellion was finally suppressed three years later in Ulster, and the future existence of the rebel leaders hung by a precarious thread.

Three years later, in September of 1607 and in what is known as The Flight of the Earls, Hugh O'Neill, 2nd Earl of Tyrone and Rory O'Donnell, 1st Earl of Tyrconnel, sailed into foreign exile from the village of Rathmullan, on the shore of Lough Swilly, Donegal, accompanied by ninety loyal followers.

For many, this marked the collapse of the centuries-old Gaelic order.

The McDermotts of Moylurg paid dearly for their part in the rebellion, with vast swathes of their territory confiscated by the Crown – but even worse was to follow.

In an insurrection that exploded in 1641, at least 2,000 Protestant settlers were massacred at the hands of Catholic landowners and their native Irish peasantry, while thousands more were stripped of their belongings and driven from their lands to seek refuge where they could.

Terrible as the atrocities were against the Protestant settlers, subsequent accounts became greatly exaggerated, serving to fuel a burning desire on the part of Protestants for revenge against the rebels.

Tragically for Ireland, this revenge became directed not only against the rebels, but native Irish Catholics such as the McDermotts in general.

The English Civil War intervened to prevent immediate action against the rebels, but following the execution of Charles I in 1649 and the consolidation of the power of England's fanatically Protestant Oliver Cromwell, the time was ripe for revenge.

The Lord Protector, as he was named, descended on Ireland at the head of a 20,000-strong army that landed at Ringford, near Dublin, in August of 1649.

The consequences of this Cromwellian conquest still resonate throughout the island today.

Cromwell had three main aims: to quash all forms of rebellion, to 'remove' all Catholic landowners who had taken part in the rebellion, and to convert the native Irish to the Protestant faith.

An early warning of the terrors that were in store for the native Catholic Irish came when the northeastern town of Drogheda was stormed and taken in September and between 2,000 and 4,000 of its inhabitants killed, including priests who were summarily put to the sword.

The defenders of Drogheda's St. Peter's Church were burned to death as they huddled for refuge in the steeple and the church was deliberately torched.

In Wexford, on the southeast coast, at least 1,500 of its inhabitants were slaughtered, including 200 defenceless women, despite their pathetic pleas for mercy.

Three hundred other inhabitants of the town drowned when their overladen boats sank as they desperately tried to flee to safety, while a group of Franciscan friars were massacred in their church.

Cromwell soon held Ireland in a grip of iron, allowing him to implement what amounted to a policy of ethnic cleansing.

His troopers were given free rein to hunt down and kill priests, while all Catholic estates, such as those of the McDermotts of Moylurg, were confiscated.

While the McDermotts of Moylurg were all but destroyed their kinsfolk, the McDermott Roe, had thrived and managed to retain their lands.

This had been through a judicious, but often dangerous, policy of seeking an accommodation with the powerful forces of the English Crown, and ruling as Lords of Tir Tuathail, in the north east of present day Co. Roscommon.

Other lands were held, including in Co. Sligo, and in 1669 it was arranged for the dispossessed McDermotts of Moylurg to receive the McDermott Roe barony known as Coolavin, on the north shore of Loch Gara.

This remained their seat until the late 1800s, with the Chief of the Name recognised as Prince of Coolavin – a title retained today by Rory McDermot who, as Chief of the Name at the time of writing, is styled 'The MacDermot, Prince of Coolavin.'

While some members of the McDermott Roe sept converted to the Protestant faith, others retained their

Catholicism, with one son of the line becoming Roman Catholic Bishop of Ardagh.

The family also acted as patron to the great Irish composer Turlough O'Carolan, born in 1670, and who performed a vital service in preserving for posterity the ancient Irish musical tradition.

In later centuries one McDermott in particular played a leading role in Ireland's struggle for independence from Britain.

This was Séan McDermott, born in Co. Leitrim in 1883, and one of the leaders of the Easter Rising of 1916, known in Gaelic as Éiri Amach na Cásca.

MacDermott was a member of the supreme council of the Irish Republican Brotherhood (I.R.B.) that, in 1916, allied itself with the Irish Citizen Army (I.C.A) with the aim of wresting independence from Britain by force of arms.

He had been arrested in May of 1915 under the terms of the Defence of the Realm Act for delivering a speech against enlistment in the British Army, then engaged in the carnage of the First World War.

Released in September, he then became involved in the planning of the Rising.

On April 24, Easter Monday, following the posting of a proclamation of independence, the combined republican forces of the I.C.A. and the I.R.B. seized strategic locations throughout Dublin, including the General Post Office.

Handicapped by polio, McDermott could take no active

part in the actual fighting, but co-ordinated military activity from the headquarters the rebels had set up in the post office.

Other Risings were timed to take place simultaneously throughout the counties of Galway, Wexford, and Louth.

With a force of less than 5,000 republicans matched against no less than 16,000 well armed and trained troops and 1,000 armed police, the Rising was doomed to failure – coming to a bloody and exhausted conclusion on April 30 after its leaders were forced into reluctant surrender.

More than 1,200 republicans, troops, police, and civilians had been killed, but further deaths followed as the sixteen leaders of the Rising, including McDermott, were executed by firing squad in the grounds of Dublin's Kilmainham Jail.

Séan MacDermott Street in Dublin is named in honour, in addition to MacDiarmada railway station in Sligo, and Pááirc Sean MacDiarmada – the Gaelic Athletic Association stadium in Carrick-on-Shannon.

Chapter four:

On the world stage

Bearers of the McDermott surname, in all its rich variety of spellings, have gained celebrity at an international level in a diverse range of pursuits.

Born in 1961 in Waterbury, Connecticut, **Dylan McDermott** is the American film and television actor whose movie roles include the 1987 Vietnam War drama *Hamburger Hill*, the 1989 *Steel Magnolias*, and the 1993 *In the Line of Fire*.

His television roles have included *Ally McBeal*, *Will and Grace*, and the legal drama *The Practice*.

Born in Carnoustie, Angus, in 1944, **Ian McDiarmid** is the noted stage, film, and television actor who has also directed a number of plays.

His best known role is as Palpatine in the *Star Wars* series of movies, while he also had memorable roles in the 1983 *Gorky Park*, and the 1999 *Sleepy Hollow*, that also starred Johnny Depp.

He won a coveted Tony Award in 2006 for Best Featured Actor for his role in the play *Faith Healer*.

Paul McDermott, born in Adelaide in 1962, is the Australian musical comedian who, as a member of the former *Doug Anthony All Stars*, first achieved international comic fame appearing in such diverse festivals as the

Adelaide Fringe Festival and the Edinburgh Fringe Festival.

Following the disbandment of the *Doug Anthony All Stars*, McDermott went on to write, direct, and perform in the celebrated stage show *MOSH!*

In the world of music **John McDermott**, born in 1955 in Glasgow and who immigrated with his family to Canada in 1965, is the famed tenor best known for his haunting rendition of the famous Irish ballad *Danny Boy* that he first recorded in 1992.

In addition to singing anthems at the Toronto Blue Jays and Toronto Maple Leafs games between 1988 and 1992, he also memorably performed at ceremonies in France in 1995 to mark the 50th anniversary of the D-Day landings.

Born Gilbert Hastings MacDermott in 1845 Islington, London, but better known as **G.H. Hastings**, or 'the Great McDermott', this theatrical agent and music hall manager found fame as the singer of 'The Jingo War Song', through which the British patriotic term 'Jingoism' first entered the language.

MacDermott, who died in 1901, was also famed for his rendition of the popular song 'Champagne Charlie.'

In the world of the printed word **Alice McDermott**, born in 1957 in Brooklyn, New York, is the author who has been a finalist for the prestigious Pulitzer Prize on no less than three occasions – in 2006 for *After This: A Novel*, and the 1992 *At Weddings and Cakes*.

She won America's National Book Award in 1998 for her novel *Charming Billy*.

Born in 1955 in Kirkcaldy, Fife, **Val McDermid** is the Scottish crime novelist, Oxford University graduate, and former journalist known for her best selling Lindsay Gordon Mysteries, Kate Brannigan Mysteries, and Tony Hill and Carol Jordan Novels.

A winner in 1997 of the Crime Writers' Association Gold Dagger Award for Best Crime Novel of the Year, her Tony Hill and Carol Jordan novels have been successfully adapted for television under the title of *Wire in the Blood*.

Born in 1941 in Detroit, **Gerald McDermott** is the American filmmaker, illustrator, and author of children's books. He won the prestigious Caldecott Honor medal in 1972 for his book *Anansi the Spider*, based on an African folktale, while he was also a recipient of the medal three years later for his book *Arrow to the Sun*.

A poet who wrote in both English and literary Scots, Christopher Murray Grieve, born in 1892 in Langholm, Dumfriesshire and who died in 1978, was better known under his pen name of **Hugh McDiarmid**.

Recognised as one of the most significant poets of the twentieth century he was also both a communist and a Scottish nationalist. His best-known work was *A Drunk Man Looks at the Thistle*, written in 1926.

In the world of science **Alan MacDiarmid**, born in 1927 in Masterton, New Zealand, and who died in 2007, was the chemist who was one of the three recipients of the Nobel Prize for Chemistry in 2000.

This was in recognition of his groundbreaking research, along with the American physicist Alan Heeger and the Japanese chemist Hideki Shirakawa, into plastic materials that can conduct electricity.

Born in 1896, **John McDermott** was the Northern Irish lawyer and politician who served as Lord Chief Justice of Northern Ireland from 1951 to 1971, eight years before his death.

He was made a life peer as Baron MacDermott in 1947.

Also in the world of politics **John McDiarmid**, born in 1882 in Perthshire, Scotland, and who immigrated to Canada with his family when he was aged five, was the Manitoba politician who served as Lieutenant-Governor of Manitoba from 1953 to 1960. He died in 1965.

In the highly competitive world of sport **Bobby McDermott**, born in 1914 in Queens, New York and who died in 1963, was the professional basketball player who during his playing career was known as the greatest long-distance shooter in the history of the game. Teams he played for included the Brooklyn Visitations, Original Celtics, Fort Wayne Zollner Pistons, and Chicago Gears. He was named to the Basketball Hall of Fame in 1988.

On the baseball field **Terry McDermott**, born in 1951 in New York, was the first baseman in Major League Baseball who played for the Los Angeles Dodgers.

Mickey McDermott, born in 1929 in Poughkeepsie, New York, and who died in 2003, was the left-handed pitcher who played for teams that included Boston Red Sox, Washington Senators, New York Yankees, Kansas City Athletes, Detroit Tigers, and St. Louis Cardinals.

On the ice rink **Terry McDermott**, born in 1940 in Essexville, Michigan, is the former American speed skater who took the gold medal for the 500 metres at the 1964 Winter Olympics in Innsbruck and won a silver at the 1968 Winter Olympics in Grenoble.

He was inducted into the National Speedskating Hall of Fame in 1977.

In the world of European football **Terence McDermott**, born in 1951 in Kirby, Merseyside is the former midfielder who played for Liverpool in the 1970s and 1980s.

His son **Neale McDermott**, born in 1985 in Newcastle, is also a midfielder who, at the time of writing, plays for Carlisle United.

Born in 1961 in Slough, Berkshire, **Brian McDermott** is the English footballer and coach who played for teams that included Arsenal, Fulham, Oxford United, Huddersfield Town, Cardiff City, and Exeter City.

At the time of writing he is reserve team manager and chief scout at Reading Football Club.

On the golf course **John J. McDermott**, born in 1891 in Philadelphia and who died in 1971, was the golfer who won the U.S. Open in 1911, at the Chicago Golf Club, making him the first American-born golfer to do so and also the youngest U.S. Open champion of all time.

He retained his title the following year, at the Country Club of Buffalo, in New York State, shooting 294 for four rounds on a par 74 course, making him the first golfer to break par for 72 holes.

Tragedy struck him in 1914 when he visited Britain to compete in the British Open, but arrived too late to play.

On his return home across the Atlantic his ship collided with another vessel and he was among a number of passengers who spent a considerable amount of time in a lifeboat before being rescued.

He began to suffer from blackouts shortly afterwards and never played golf again, spending the rest of his life suffering from mental illness.

On the battlefield **Robert F. McDermott**, born in 1920 in Boston, is regarded in American military circles as 'the father of modern military education.'

Serving as a combat pilot and operations officer during the Second World War and as a staff officer in the Pentagon, he was a recipient of the Bronze Star, the Air Medal with five oak leaf clusters, the European Theater of Operations Ribbon with six battle stars, the Distinguished Service Medal, and the Legion of Merit.

President Dwight D. Eisenhower personally appointed him in 1957 as the first permanent professor of the United States Air Force Academy, and two years later as its first permanent Dean of the Faculty, with the promotion to Brigadier General. He died in 2006.

Key dates in Ireland's history from the first settlers to the formation of the Irish Republic:

circa 7000 B.C.	Arrival and settlement of Stone Age people.
circa 3000 B.C.	Arrival of settlers of New Stone Age period.
circa 600 B.C.	First arrival of the Celts.
200 A.D.	Establishment of Hill of Tara, Co. Meath, as seat of the High Kings.
circa 432 A.D.	Christian mission of St. Patrick.
800-920 A.D.	Invasion and subsequent settlement of Vikings.
1002 A.D.	Brian Boru recognised as High King.
1014	Brian Boru killed at battle of Clontarf.
1169-1170	Cambro-Norman invasion of the island.
1171	Henry II claims Ireland for the English Crown.
1366	Statutes of Kilkenny ban marriage between native Irish and English.
1529-1536	England's Henry VIII embarks on religious Reformation.
1536	Earl of Kildare rebels against the Crown.
1541	Henry VIII declared King of Ireland.
1558	Accession to English throne of Elizabeth I.
1565	Battle of Affane.
1569-1573	First Desmond Rebellion.
1579-1583	Second Desmond Rebellion.
1594-1603	Nine Years War.
1606	Plantation' of Scottish and English settlers.

1607	Flight of the Earls.
1632-1636	Annals of the Four Masters compilcd.
1641	Rebellion over policy of plantation and other grievances.
1649	Beginning of Cromwellian conquest.
1688	Flight into exile in France of Catholic Stuart monarch James II as Protestant Prince William of Orange invited to take throne of England along with his wife, Mary.
1689	William and Mary enthroned as joint monarchs; siege of Derry.
1690	Jacobite forces of James defeated by William at battle of the Boyne (July) and Dublin taken.
1691	Athlone taken by William; Jacobite defeats follow at Aughrim, Galway, and Limerick; conflict ends with Treaty of Limerick (October) and Irish officers allowed to leave for France.
1695	Penal laws introduced to restrict rights of Catholics; banishment of Catholic clergy.
1704	Laws introduced constricting rights of Catholics in landholding and public office.
1728	Franchise removed from Catholics.
1791	Foundation of United Irishmen republican movement.
1796	French invasion force lands in Bantry Bay.
1798	Defeat of Rising in Wexford and death of United Irishmen leaders Wolfe Tone and Lord Edward Fitzgerald.

1800	Act of Union between England and Ireland.
1803	Dublin Rising under Robert Emmet.
1829	Catholics allowed to sit in Parliament.
1845-1849	The Great Hunger: thousands starve to death as potato crop fails and thousands more emigrate.
1856	Phoenix Society founded.
1858	Irish Republican Brotherhood established.
1873	Foundation of Home Rule League.
1893	Foundation of Gaelic League.
1904	Foundation of Irish Reform Association.
1913	Dublin strikes and lockout.
1916	Easter Rising in Dublin and proclamation of an Irish Republic.
1917	Irish Parliament formed after Sinn Fein election victory.
1919-1921	War between Irish Republican Army and British Army.
1922	Irish Free State founded, while six northern counties remain part of United Kingdom as Northern Ireland, or Ulster; civil war up until 1923 between rival republican groups.
1949	Foundation of Irish Republic after all remaining constitutional links with Britain are severed.